D0487789

GARDEN GUIDES

THE WATER GARDEN

GARDEN GUIDES

THE WATER GARDEN

LANCE HATTATT

Illustrations by
ELAINE FRANKS
and
BRENDA STEPHENSON

A Siena book.
Siena is an imprint of Parragon Books.

This edition first published in 1996 by
Parragon Book Service Ltd
Unit 13–17, Avonbridge Trading Estate
Atlantic Road
Avonmouth
Bristol BS11 9QD

Produced by
Robert Ditchfield Ltd
Combe Court
Kerry's Gate
Hereford HR2 0AH

ISBN 0 75251 600 0

A copy of the British Library Cataloguing in Publication Data is available from the Library.

The illustrations on pages 18, 19, 20, 21 and 64 are by Brenda Stephenson. All other illustrations are by Elaine Franks.

Typeset by Action Typesetting Ltd, Gloucester
Colour origination by Mandarin Offset Ltd, Hong Kong
Printed and bound in Italy

ACKNOWLEDGEMENTS

Many of the photographs were taken in the author's garden, Arrow Cottage, Ledgemoor, Weobley. The publishers would also like to thank the many people and organizations who have allowed photographs to be taken for this book, including the following:

Mr and Mrs Terence Aggett; Mrs Anthony Anderson; Lucinda Aldrich-Blake; Aspects Garden Design, Brampton Abbotts, Ross-on-Wye; Bromesberrow Place; Burford House, Tenbury Wells; Cheltenham Landscape Company; The Country Garden Centre, Huntley; Lallie Cox, Woodpeckers, Marlcliff, Bidford-on-Avon; Denmans, Chichester; Dinmore Manor; Richard Edwards, Well Cottage, Blakemere; Field House, Clee St. Margaret; Mrs G.A. Follis; Frampton Manor; Lance Hattatt, Arrow Cottage, Weobley; Haseley Court; The Hon Mrs Peter Healing, The Priory, Kemerton; Hill Court; Mrs R. Humphries, Orchard Bungalow, Bishops Frome; Great Dixter; Mr Milton Grundy; Oxford Botanic Garden; Mrs R. Paice, Bourton House; Mr D. Pyecroft; Mrs Clive Richards, Lower Hope, Ullingswick; Mary-Ann Robinson; Royal Botanic Gardens, Kew; RHS Garden, Wisley; Snowshill (National Trust); Malley Terry, 28 Hillgrove Crescent, Kidderminster; Raymond Treasure, Stockton Bury Farm, Kimbolton; Mrs Trevor-Jones, Preen Manor; Richard Walker; Webbs of Wychbold; Mrs Geoffrey Williams, Close Farm, Crockham Hill; Mrs David Williams-Thomas, The Manor House, Birlingham; Woodlands, Bridstow; York Gate, Leeds.

We would like to thank especially Kenchester Water Gardens, Hereford for their help in this project. We would also like to thank Stapeley Water Gardens Ltd., London Road, Stapeley, Nantwich, Cheshire for their kind permission to reproduce photographs of *Nymphaea* 'Sioux', 'Mme Wilfon Gonnère', 'Graziella', 'Venusta', 'Rosennymphe', 'Gonnère', 'Odorata Sulphurea', *Stratiotes aloides, Nymphoides peltata, Azolla caroliniana*, goldfish, sea-lion, bell fountain, fountain bowl and Tiffany water features.

CONTENTS

Poisonous Plants

In recent years, concern has been voiced about poisonous plants or plants which can cause allergic reactions if touched. The fact is that many plants are poisonous, some in a particular part, others in all their parts. For the sake of safety, it is always, without exception, essential to assume that no part of a plant should be eaten unless it is known, without any doubt whatsoever, that the plant or its part is edible and that it cannot provoke an allergic reaction in the individual person who samples it. It must also be remembered that some plants can cause severe dermatitis, blistering or an allergic reaction if touched, in some individuals and not in others. It is the responsibility of the individual to take all the above into account.

Water in the Garden

All water gardens are beautiful, but sadly they can be dangerous, mostly to children who can drown in even a few inches of water, or sometimes to adults. We would urge readers where necessary to take account of this and provide a reliable means of protection if they include water in the garden.

How to Use This Book

Where appropriate, approximate measurements of a plant's height have been given, and also the spread where this is significant, in both metric and imperial measures. The height is the first measurement, as for example 1.2m × 60cm/4 × 2ft. However, both height and spread vary so greatly from garden to garden since they depend on soil, climate and position, that these measurements are offered as guides only. This is especially true of trees and shrubs where ultimate growth can be unpredictable.

The following symbols are also used throughout the book:

- ❍ = thrives best or only in full sun
- ◐ = thrives best or only in part-shade
- ● = succeeds in full shade
- E = evergreen

Where no sun symbol and no reference to sun or shade is made in the text, it can be assumed that the plant tolerates sun or light shade.

Plant Names

For ease of reference this book gives the botanical name under which a plant is most widely listed for the gardener. These names are sometimes changed and in such cases the new name has been included. Common names are given wherever they are in frequent use.

The Water Garden

From the simplest of trickling spouts poised to splash into a stone basin to the dignified serenity of a lake, water in the garden has an irresistible, magical quality. For some people it is the sound of a babbling brook, for others the movement of a fast flowing river, whilst for others it is the peace to be found in the stillness of a pond.

Few are fortunate enough to possess a natural water feature within the garden. For most this aquatic desire has to be satisfied by creating some element which will not only complement the surrounding environment but which can also be realized within the strict limitations of a budget.

Formal and Informal Effects

The introduction of some form of water into the garden will, to a large degree, depend upon the existing layout of borders, lawns and paths as well as the space available. Obviously it would be both impracticable and foolish to attempt a lake within the confines of a small, town garden as it would be absurd

A charming small water garden on a sloping site.

A formal pool with cascades makes a dramatic feature in this large garden.

to place a squat, bell fountain as a centrepiece in parkland. Scale, as with all things outdoors, is vitally important.

Where the garden is designed along lines of formality, then a classic pool of symmetrical shape, rill or even canal would suggest themselves. Surrounded by quality stone paving and minimal but carefully chosen planting, the effect can be stunning. A wall mask, perhaps of a traditional lion's head, the mouthpiece acting as a water outlet, an antique cistern or an ornate fountain would all be suitable in a formal situation.

In a freer, more natural setting an irregularly shaped pond or rippling stream would be a charming addition to the garden scene. In such instances planting should be exuberant, a profusion of flowers and foliage. For a cottage garden look, a wooden barrel filled with water could be positioned in a shady corner together with an old-fashioned pump for added authenticity. On a rockery a small water course with a series of carefully contrived falls would not look out of place.

Planting A Water Garden

Giving plants suitable and appropriate growing conditions in the garden is important if they are to succeed and perform well. This is particularly so when considering planting out the water garden. Here choices must be made and decisions taken about plants which will thrive in the shallows, those which will grow in deep water, those for boggy conditions and those which simply prefer damp, moisture-retentive soil. In planning schemes these points should be borne in mind.

Water lilies, traditional surface-flowering plants for pools, have planting depths which range from as little as 10cm/4in to 1m/3ft. Other marginals, among them some grasses, reeds and rushes, will grow in shallow water of around 12.5cm/5in. The choice of plants for the bog garden, where the soil is not allowed to dry out, is wide, as is the number of plants which will enhance the areas surrounding pond or stream.

Where plants are to be submerged a suitable planting basket should be used. Readily available, these are of plastic construction with fretted sides to allow for expansion of roots. If the compost or soil to be used is light and friable, then the sides of the basket can be lined with old hessian sacking or coarse cloth to prevent spillage. Once filled containers

A natural, well planted stream in spring.

Intense greens in a garden of moisture-loving subjects.

may easily be lowered into place by means of cord or stout string passed through the upper holes.

Water Features

Plants must, of course, be the principal feature to be used in association with water. A balance between flower and leaf will need to be made, the emphasis possibly being on strong and bold foliage effects. Additionally, other design elements will come into play.

These may be an attractive bridge to span a stream, a series of stepping stones across a rivulet or a wooden landing-stage reaching out into a pond. Waterfalls and fountains, if thoughtfully sited, provide movement and interest. Commercially produced jets, water bells, bubbles and millstones will all operate by means of an electric pump and give a focal point to a patio.

Garden ornaments are many and various and pool, pond and stream accessories are no less numerous. Figures, in the form of cherubs, seraphs and mermaids, should be selected with extreme care. Likewise rules of caution should apply when contemplating the placement of storks, herons, dolphins and seals.

Goldfish, carp and orfe are all ornamental fish to decorate the pool or pond. However, all are extremely sensitive to changes in water quality, oxygen deficiency and fungal and bacterial disease. Given the right conditions they will afford hours of pleasure and be a constant source of delight.

A tiny picturesque water feature.

Water has a calming effect, acting as mirror to both sky and trees.

Care and Maintenance

Pools and ponds are subject to free-floating algae which flourish in sunlight and where there are high levels of mineral salts present in the water. To reduce this problem oxygenating plants, which absorb mineral salts and cast shade, should, according to variety, either be tossed onto the surface or submerged.

The majority of plants for the pond or water areas will die down naturally during the dormant season. Rushes with hollow stems should not be cut down below the water line, to prevent the stalks filling with water and the plant drowning. Where trees shed leaves into the water these should be collected and removed where possible to limit pollution.

Fish should not be fed in winter. At a time when ice may pose a threat it is advisable to float a rubber ball or a piece of wood on the surface of the water to reduce the pressure naturally exerted by the ice. In severe conditions a pan of boiling water placed on the surface will melt through the ice to release any toxic gases which may have built up.

During the colder months it is worth disconnecting any pumps to be serviced, cleaned and stored in readiness for the coming season. Periodically ponds and pools should be emptied to allow for thorough cleaning and routine maintenance work.

1. Ponds

Reflections, showy plantings, ripples on water, wildlife and the warmth of the summer sun are the very being of a pond.

Making *a* Pond

Siting a Pond

Within a garden situation a pond needs to blend in with its surroundings to appear, as far as possible, at one with nature.

A low point in the garden should be chosen, and one which allows room for generous marginal plantings.

A site enjoying a good measure of sunlight will ensure that both fish and aquatic plants thrive. The proximity of deciduous trees and shrubs will make for unwanted shade, whilst fallen leaves left to rot on the bottom of the pond will release harmful gases.

Caught in a moment of bright sunshine, this well-sited garden pool looks particularly inviting.

Few gardens need be without a natural looking pond. Positioned in a secluded, quiet corner or as a dominant feature, it breathes life into the garden creating atmosphere, mood and character. With the availability of quality liners or preformed shapes the installation of a pond is not a daunting prospect. Once installed it becomes a near fixture. It is, therefore, necessary to position it correctly from both an aesthetic and horticultural point of view.

This shallow little pond is thoughtfully edged with drifts of primula and moisture-loving ferns.

Plantings here have been deliberately chosen to provide a contrast of texture and form.

Simplicity is the keynote here. A clear expanse of water echoes the gravel before the house.

Flag iris, rushes and large-leaved foliage plants surround this peaceful pond. Lush plantings mask the edges generating visual interest as well as giving cover for wildlife. The unplanted water surface allows for attractive reflections to be seen.

Making *a* Pond

Carefully positioned stone edging follows the line of the hedge which encloses this pond garden.

This pool garden relies heavily upon sweeps of close planting to achieve its effect.

Closely mown grass borders one side of this pond. In comparison the other is thickly planted.

Positioned within a walled garden where the heat is trapped, this beautifully planted pond forms a cool oasis.

Bold plantings of *Alchemilla mollis* mask this pond's edge whilst the royal fern (*Osmunda regalis*) adds contrast of form.

A great sense of peace and calm is achieved in this attractively planted, mature pond garden.

◆ *Conifers give scale and make for year-round interest.*

MAKING *a* POND

POOL LINERS ARE A FLEXIBLE METHOD of creating a pond to almost any size and shape. Although a number of cheaper liners, such as polythene and PVC, are on the market, the initial outlay for a quality rubber or butyl liner will more than repay itself for its appearance and durability.

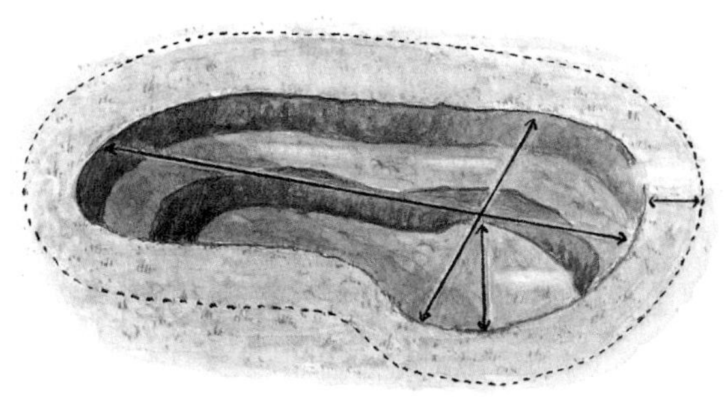

MEASURING THE POND

Irregularly shaped pools should be treated as rectangles for the purpose of measuring. The measurements to be taken are: length, width, depth and overlap (the overlap is the amount of liner required to secure it firmly to the ground – approximately 45cm/1½ft). The quantity of liner needed will be:
(2 × depth + length + 2 × overlap) × (2 × depth + width + 2 × overlap)

EXCAVATING THE SITE

Dig out the pool to the desired shape and size. Remove any sticks or stones likely to puncture or damage the liner. Cover the base of the pond and the marginal planting shelves with a layer of sand to a depth of 2.5cm/1in. This will afford the liner added protection. Wads of saturated newspaper may be used to line the sides.

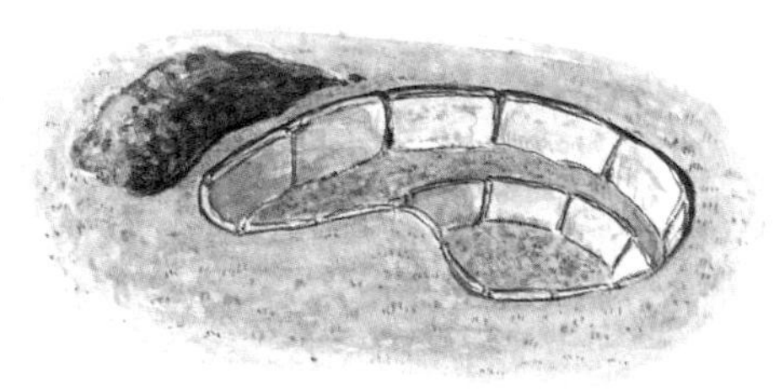

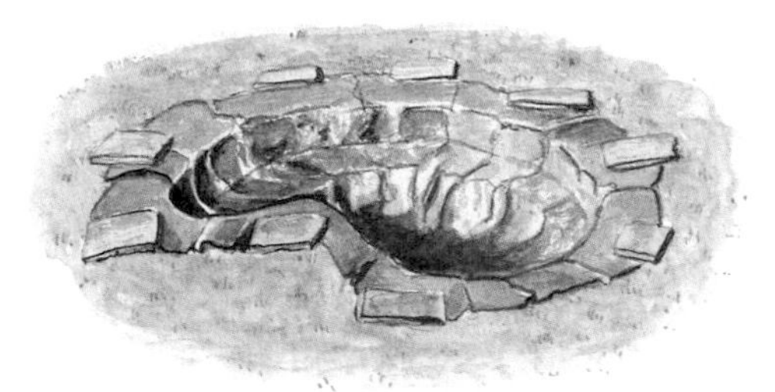

PLACING THE LINER

The butyl liner should be stretched over the excavated pond. Slabs or bricks may be used at this stage to secure the liner in place in readiness for filling with water.

Filling the Pond

As the pond begins to fill, major creases should be pulled out. Once full, surplus edging material may be cut away, but you will need to ensure that sufficient overlap remains, which you can conceal under edging slabs.

Finishing Off

Because of the non-toxic quality of pool liners, the pond may be put into immediate use. Plants may be added and fish, if required, may be introduced.

A kidney shaped pond made with a liner. A rock feature on one side has allowed the designer to incorporate a waterfall.

◆ *Note how well the pond is landscaped into the garden with both plantings and hard materials.*

MAKING *a* POND

PUDDLED CLAY IS THE ULTIMATE in pond linings but it is a specialist technique requiring appropriate soil and conditions. Most people are content to use either a butyl liner or a ready-made shape. Moulded ponds are available generally in weather-resistant plastic or fibreglass. They are not made in very large sizes but are a sensible choice for a small rock pool or a feature in a small garden.

INSTALLING A PREFORMED POND

1. Excavate a large, rectangular hole which, when complete, will comfortably accommodate the pond. This hole will be greater than the length, width and depth of the pond to allow for adequate backfilling.

2. Spread a layer of sand to a depth of 2.5cm/1in across the bottom of the hole. Install the pond, supporting it where necessary with wedges which will later be removed as backfilling takes place. The pond should be set at least 2.5cm/1in below ground level to allow for any lifting.

3. Check with a spirit level and commence backfilling. Continue at intervals to check that the pond is level. Firm soil around the pond to eliminate air pockets.

4. Add water whilst backfilling continues. This should result in a stable, level pond. Once full, planting may take place and the disturbed surroundings can be restored.

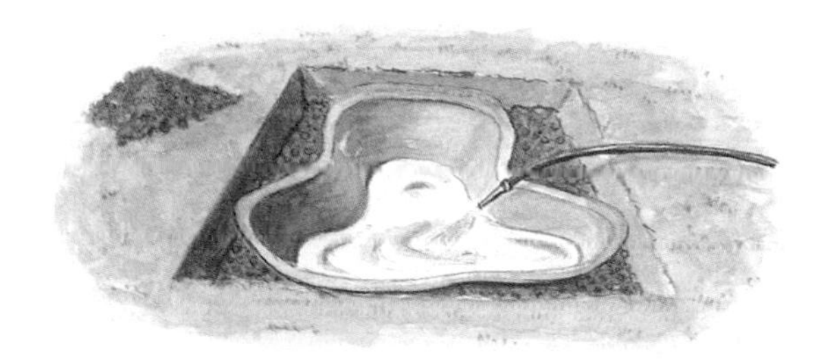

Preformed pools are ideal for even the smallest gardens. This one has been concealed beneath a naturalistic setting of slate rocks.

◆ *The water-spout is powered by an electric pump.*

Modern plastics are designed to withstand extremes of weather and will not crack or split under the rigours of routine maintenance. Most ponds are manufactured to acquire a natural appearance within a short space of time.

Making *a* Pond

Some gardens simply do not have space for a pond of any real size. However, it is still possible to include a small feature in the form of a sunken barrel, tank, trough or suitable container, all of which can be adapted to hold water.

Colour is deliberately restricted here to heighten the visual impact of the whole.

This inviting area could well be termed a pool patio. Water, hard and soft landscaping are given equal weight.

◆ *Garden ornaments need not be expensive. Good, reasonably priced reproductions are easily obtained.*

Pebble pools such as this one are not difficult to construct and make a pleasing feature.

This tiny pond is the very heart and focal point of imaginative, massed planting.

MAKING *a* POND

A wall spout is used here above stone troughs to create an interesting, effective water feature.

Nothing could be simpler than this metal basin used as a container for water lilies.

A simple treatment of water which could be adapted to many garden situations.

This arrangement of mask, trough and lead-type urns shows how a completely symmetrical arrangement can be broken to advantage by the use of plants. The lion mask, centrally placed, is allowed to just peek out from his ivy hiding-place. The variegated grass in the trough is encouraged to romp. In this way, a small formal picture has become more relaxed.

Lysichiton americanus Skunk cabbages are good spring marginals. 1m × 75cm/3 × 2½ft

◆ *Yellow spathes are followed by huge leaves.*

Caltha palustris The marsh marigold's flowers are carried above dark green leaves. ❍, 30 × 45cm/ 1 × 1½ft

◆ *Ideal for edging ponds.*

***Caltha palustris* 'Flore Pleno'** is a double form of the marsh marigold forming splendid clumps. ❍, 30 × 30cm/1 × 1ft

Lysichiton camtschatcensis boasts a white spathe. They are easily raised from seed but take some years to flower. 75 × 60cm/2½ × 2ft

***Zantedeschia aethiopica* 'Crowborough'** A spectacular plant whose white flowers are stunning. 60 × 60/2 × 2ft

***Geum rivale* 'Album'** (Water avens) is unfussy about situation but looks very effective with marginal plants. 60 × 60cm/2 × 2ft

Marginal Plantings

Exciting results are achieved when plants of differing form and texture are used at the margins of the pond. As well as concealing any unsightly or awkward edges, marginals act as a link between aquatic plants growing in the water and those which are established at the pondside.

Growing in the shallows at the pond's edge is the handsome, North American pickerel weed, ***Pontederia cordata***, its shaped foliage contrasting with that of ***Iris laevigata***. Creeping along the edges is the cheerful little hybrid **mimulus**. This obliging small perennial is not particularly long lived but is easily raised from seed.

Marginal Plantings

Filipendula purpurea alba A meadowsweet splendidly at home in a waterside setting. 1.2 m × 45cm/ 4 × 1½ft

Filipendula rubra This form of meadowsweet deserves a prominent place in the pond garden. 2 × 1.2m/ 6 × 4ft

Petasites japonicus An extraordinary flower later to be followed by large leaves. Very invasive. ◐, ●, 1m/3ft × indefinite spread

Ligularia przewalskii A handsome plant producing spires of yellow flowers in late summer. 1.2 × 1m/4 × 3ft

Lysimachia punctata will rapidly colonize an area but is exceedingly useful for difficult situations. 75 × 60cm/2½ × 2ft

The size of this pond demands a bold planting scheme kept deliberately simple for maximum effect.

Persicaria (syn. ***Polygonum***) ***bistorta*** forms striking clumps of pink flowers when grown well in moist soil. 75 × 60cm/2½ × 2ft

Marginal Plantings

GIVEN THE IDEAL CONDITIONS of mud or shallow water, many strong-growing marginal plants will rapidly increase. Good gardening and careful, planned management of the pond will prevent them from becoming invasive and swamping their less vigorous companions.

Rodgersia aesculifolia must not be allowed to dry out. This is a foliage plant with attractive flowers. 1 × 1m/ 3 × 3ft

***Rodgersia pinnata* 'Superba'** An absolutely lovely form. Plant in numbers for a strong accent. 1 × 1m/3 × 3ft

Spathes of lysichiton are already showing. Later hemerocallis, trollius, iris and unusual *Senecio smithii* will flower.

Creating an Effect

There is nothing half-hearted about this marginal planting at the pond's edge. Different leaf shapes and patterns have been combined to give the whole scheme the quality of a tapestry. Colours are in harmony one with another and sufficient plants have been used to make a series of statements.

Marginal Plantings

Borders surrounding or in the vicinity of the pond need to be planted in a sympathetic manner. The transition from water to remaining garden areas should be gradual, the aim being to integrate one with another, the emphasis on naturalness. The theme of massed plantings at the water's edge may easily be extended into adjacent borders. Hemerocallis, hostas and astilbes are all striking foliage plants which, placed together in groups of three or more, will contribute shape, contrast and harmony.

Form here is as important as flower. The large, prominently marked **hosta** leaves are convincingly placed in front of the thin, strap-like foliage of the **hemerocallis**. Nearby the cut leaves and plumy flowers of ***Astilbe chinensis*** '**Pumila**' have a textural quality.

***Iris* 'Holden Clough'** is particularly effective placed in front of *Carex elata* 'Aurea'. 75 × 75cm/ 2½ × 2½ft

***Houttuynia cordata* 'Chameleon'** A showy groundcover perennial with small white flowers that spreads. ○, 10cm/4in

***Hemerocallis* 'Stella de Oro'** A most lovely day lily, forming a clump of tapering leaves. 60 × 60cm/ 2 × 2ft

***Hemerocallis* 'Bonanza'** is distinctive for yellow flowers with a deep wine-red throat. Easy in most soils. 1m × 75cm/3 × 2½ft

Trillium grandiflorum Patience is required as the beautiful wake-robin is slow to establish. ●, 38 × 30cm/ 15 × 12in

***Aruncus dioicus* 'Kneiffii'** A form of goat's beard which is not dissimilar to an astilbe. 1 × 1m/3 × 3ft

***Astilbe* 'Granat'** is not at all out of place when positioned among some of the red-hued primulas. 1 × 1m/3 × 3ft

***Astilbe* 'Deutschland'** in common with other astilbes is particularly happy in moisture-retentive soil. 1 × 1m/3 × 3ft

***Astilbe* 'Erica'** This cultivar carries plumes of soft pink. 1 × 1m/3 × 3ft

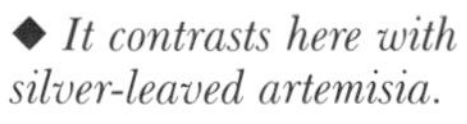

◆ *It contrasts here with silver-leaved artemisia.*

INTRODUCING FISH

Avoid tipping the fish directly into the water. Rather, allow the bag in which they were sold to float on the pond's surface until the water temperature of the bag is similar to that of the pond. Feed at once although it may be some time before the fish will appear regularly for feeding. To begin with, their inclination will be to hide.

◆ *These young fish are ready for sale. Look for stiff, erect fins and general liveliness.*

The **common goldfish**, a member of the carp family, is the most popular of all fish for the garden pool. It is hardy, surviving even bad winters outside, though it needs water at least 45cm/1½ft in at least a part of its pond. It breeds easily, though not until it has reached a length of about 12.5cm/5in.

WINTER WEATHER

Fish will survive winter months without feeding, their body processes slowing down to adjust to the cold. In prolonged icy weather, surface ice may be melted by holding a container of boiling water on the pond. This will release any harmful gases trapped under the ice that could harm the fish. Never resort to more violent methods of breaking ice.

REGULAR FEEDING

A correctly balanced pond that is not over-populated with fish will contain sufficient nutrients in the form of aquatic life to sustain health and vigour. However, feeding fish with a good proprietary brand of food will do no harm. Fish are not greedy feeders. Only small amounts of food should be given at any one time. When colder weather sets in, feeding should cease.

FISH

FOR MANY, A POND WITHOUT FISH is incomplete. Indeed, ornamental fish do provide a decorative element in the water garden as well as helping to control some of the insect pests to be found in and around water. The most popular choice remains goldfish, with bronze carp coming a close second. Additionally, shubunkins, common carp, orfe, rudd and roach will all live happily side by side in the larger pond.

Feeding fish at the same time and in the same place will establish a routine to which they will become accustomed.

The **Koi carp**, the most exotic of the hardy cold water fish, is a beautiful creature with a chunky head and body. Some have brilliant metallic scales of orange or red.

◆ *They grow quickly and are suited to pools of over 10.5 sq.m/35 sq.ft and with a depth of at least 1m/3ft.*

Wildlife

GARDEN PONDS PROVIDE AN EXCELLENT HABITAT for many forms of wildlife. Frogs and toads not only add interest but are greatly beneficial as they feed on harmful insects and slugs. Newts, with their colourful underbodies, frequent the pond during the summer months, a time for dragonflies and damsels. Stones placed at the pond's edge allow wildlife ease of access to and from the water.

Coping with Herons

Fish within a pond are, unfortunately, prey to herons. These imposing birds are at large in the early morning when their activities are least likely to be disturbed.

To prevent this nuisance, ponds may be covered with plastic netting or surrounded with short canes supporting black thread or fishing line.

In this situation a decoy heron has been placed at the water's edge among marginal plantings. Live herons will, in theory, be discouraged in the face of opposition.

Newts are to be found in water only for short periods during which time they mate and lay their eggs. For the rest of the year they live under stones, hibernating in winter.

Frogs, and indeed toads, should be encouraged and welcomed into the garden for they are of enormous benefit in reducing all manner of garden pests.

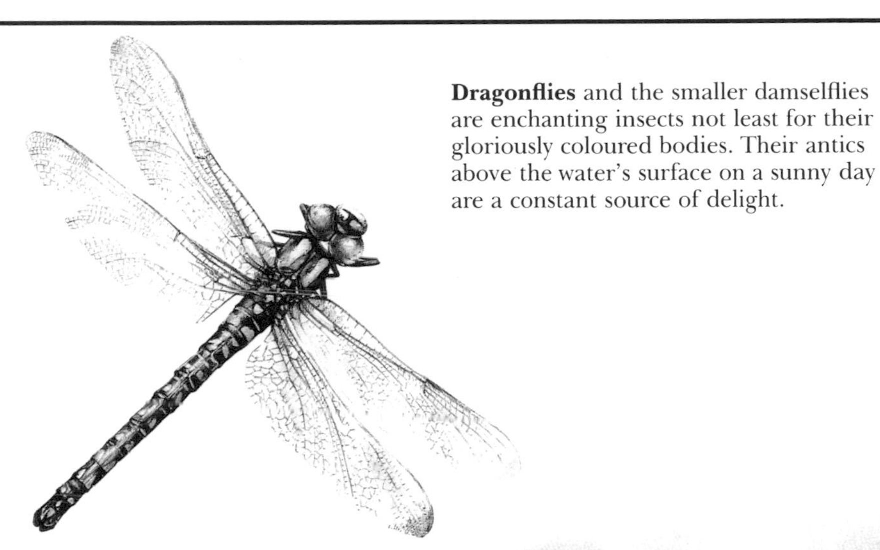

Dragonflies and the smaller damselflies are enchanting insects not least for their gloriously coloured bodies. Their antics above the water's surface on a sunny day are a constant source of delight.

Wild ducks may be attracted to large ponds at certain times of the year. Apart from muddying up the water they present no real problem as they are unlikely to remain in the garden situation for very long.

2. Formal Pools

The straight lines or geometrical curves of a formal water feature suggest style and sophistication in even the smallest of gardens.

DESIGNING *a* POOL

SURROUNDING THE POOL

The materials chosen to surround the formal pool will be important in determining the overall effect.

Quality paving, in the form of reclaimed flags, is expensive but well worth the initial investment. Likewise old bricks or setts, arranged according to a traditional pattern, will create an immediate impression of maturity and timelessness.

SPACE, the use of compatible materials and restrained, co-ordinated plantings are the necessary ingredients of a formal water scheme. Designs succeed best where they can be tied in to some existing structure: a walled court, a sunken garden, a terrace, an enclosure.

A raised pool such as this one would not be too difficult to achieve, for it involves little excavation.

This antique pool of basket-weave design is set in a formal area of lawn and box parterre.

Straight lines are repeated to good effect in this raised canal, path and well trimmed hedge.

An attractive and intimate court well clothed with stylish plantings making good use of minimal colour.

◆ *The open gate at the top of the steps invites further exploration of the garden.*

DESIGNING *a* POOL

Modern reproductions of old style materials will soon acquire a weathered look. Sour milk, or yoghurt, painted on surfaces will speed this process.

An excellent use of water, stone and green foliage plants to give an air of understated elegance.

Clipped ivy and box mask the construction of this above-ground rectangular pool. Planting in the water is minimal.

This brick water feature becomes an extension of the wall behind to provide total harmony.

This pool is the centrepiece of an enclosed, brightly coloured water garden.

Much thought and good judgment have been applied to the arrangement and planting of this pool.

Symmetry and formality combine by aligning the centre of the pool with that of the door and by the placing of the planters.

◆ *Blue paint used here on the furniture and containers is much more sympathetic than white would have been.*

DESIGNING *a* POOL

DRAWING OUT A PLAN TO SCALE will eliminate mistakes at an early stage and before serious construction work gets under way. Generous proportions guarantee a result which is pleasing to the eye. An arrangement of pots will enhance formality.

A well placed seat, strategically sited pots and a canopy of trees call for a moment's pause in a city garden.

◆ *The lush plantings associated with water create a cool, calm atmosphere.*

A charming pavilion is positioned to act as an eye-catcher at the end of this lily pond.

Roughly shaped rocks are used as a substantial edging to this water effect.

DESIGNING *a* POOL

Close planting and the proximity of the wall convey a sense of intimacy in this shady enclosure.

Large slabs of a uniform size have been used to edge this shaped pool.

Sophisticated use of a small place where box pyramids overlook a pebbled rectangle with a central water bubble.

Although this pool is rather grandly placed, the ideas of symmetry, formality and space may be introduced elsewhere.

Care has been taken to line up the centre of the pool with the archway leading to another part of the garden.

Three simple cascades contribute interest as well as the sound of water in this raised, stone pool.

◆ *Though part of a larger pool, this structure could easily be built in a small garden.*

FLOATING *and* DEEP WATER PLANTS

FEW THINGS ARE LESS APPEALING than the sight of a pool which is the consistency of pea soup and overrun with blanket weed. Floating and submerged oxygenating plants will, to a great extent, minimize these conditions and promote healthy, clear water. Some of these plants are chosen for a specific purpose, to fulfil a role, and are therefore not especially decorative. However, others will produce flowers and be pretty in their own right.

Eichhornia crassipes (Water hyacinth) floats on the surface and produces very appealing and attractive orchid-like, blue and lilac flowers.

◆ *Unfortunately the water hyacinth must be kept frost-free. Overwinter in a container of water.*

Lagarosiphon major (syn. ***Elodea crispa***) Sometimes called goldfish weed, this plant forms a spreading underwater carpet.

Pistia stratiotes is aptly named water lettuce. It should be kept indoors through the winter.

FLOATING *and* DEEP WATER PLANTS

Stratiotes aloides rather resembles a cactus plant with its spiky, sword-like leaves.

Aponogeton distachyos (Water hawthorn) has white flowers with distinctive black centres. Plant in up to 45cm/1½ft of water.

Nymphoides peltata (Water fringe) Easily mistaken for a water-lily. Plant in water up to 45cm/1½ft.

Myriophyllum aquaticum (Parrot's feather) thrives beneath the water's surface where it helps to keep water clear.

Azolla caroliniana Sometimes known as fairy moss, this plant resembles a tiny floating fern.

Orontium aquaticum possesses very striking, poker-like flowers tipped yellow.

◆ *Plant in up to 30cm/1ft of water.*

WATER LILIES

WATER LILIES, *Nymphaea*, are the most desirable, decorative and coveted of all pool plants. Shamelessly ostentatious, their brilliance cannot be ignored. Splendid waxy blooms in many lovely hues are displayed from early summer until the first frosts of autumn. They thrive in good garden soil, free from any artificial fertilizer, and should be planted either directly into the soil on the floor of the pond or into open-sided, aquatic planting baskets.

***Nymphaea* 'Laydekeri Fulgens'** Here the richly coloured fragrant flowers have spread to fill the pool. PD 23cm/9in or more

***Nymphaea* 'Sioux'** The blooms start off soft yellow and pass through orange-pink to crimson. Olive-green leaves. PD 45cm/1½ft

***Nymphaea* 'Mme Wilfon Gonnère'** Almost fully double cup-shaped flowers, 15cm/6in across. PD 45cm/1½ft

***Nymphaea* 'Graziella'** A cup-shaped flower with rounded lobes above dark green leaves, mottled with maroon. PD 23cm/9in

PLANTING DEPTHS (PD)

Miniature lilies require no more than 23cm/9in of water whilst the small-growing varieties are happy in up to 30cm/1ft. Medium-growing lilies should have somewhere up to 45cm/1½ft of water; the most vigorous will tolerate up to 1m/3ft.

***Nymphaea* 'Venusta'** Beautifully formed flowers of warm pink, stuffed with golden stamens. PD 45cm–1m/1½–3ft

***Nymphaea* 'Rosennymphe'** Delicately coloured with pointed petals to its large flowers. PD 45cm–1m/1½–3ft

***Nymphaea* 'James Brydon'** Fragrant flowers like peonies above dark green leaves. PD 23–45cm/9in–1½ft

Water Lilies

***Nymphaea* 'Gonnère'** A fully double white water lily up to 20cm/8in across and bright green leaves. PD up to 45cm/1½ft

***Nymphaea* 'Marliacea Chromatella'** has flowers of deep yellow. Leaves, spotted brown and bronze, are olive-green. PD 45cm/1½ft

***Nymphaea odorata* 'Sulphurea Grandiflora'** has lovely fragrant blossoms. PD up to 23cm/9in

***Nymphaea* 'Escarboucle'** A vigorous water lily with flowers up to 15cm/6in, their cup filled with golden stamens. PD 1m/3ft

◆ *All water lilies will respond to division every few years in the spring.*

***Nymphaea* 'Marliacea Albida'** A pure white, scented lily with distinctive yellow stamens. PD 45cm/ 1½ft

All water lilies should be planted in full sun and still water is essential for them.

FOUNTAINS *and* WATER SPOUTS

FORMAL WATER IS ENHANCED with the addition of a sparkling fountain spray. From a single jet to myriad cascades, the constant dance and movement of water is endlessly fascinating. Whatever the design, a surface or submersible pump will ensure uninterrupted playing.

A highly imaginative yet simple water feature which is thoughtfully composed and well presented.

◆ *Even the smallest courtyard can accommodate this pot fountain.*

This handsome sea lion dominates a raised pool. Such a piece would be unsuitable in a tiny area.

FOUNTAINS *and* WATER SPOUTS

Fountains can, of course, be placed independently of a pool. Many designs exist for inclusion on a terrace, patio or even within a conservatory. Some are of classical simplicity, others incorporate figures or flowers.

Placing this delightful wall fountain would not be difficult. Its charm lies in its relative simplicity.

A charming Pan figure pipes water into the pool below in this formal setting.

Masks as water spouts are easily mounted onto a wall. A simple pump keeps water flowing.

A fountain of cupids cascading in three tiers.

FOUNTAINS *and* WATER SPOUTS

This inspired and fascinating water feature enhances a sitting out area providing a cooling effect on a hot day.

This delightful composition of figures sheltering under a water umbrella would be a point of interest anywhere.

The electric point that powers the water spout is clearly visible.

◆ *A point could be concealed behind a plant.*

Fountains such as this one would be a safer choice for families with young children.

A fountain bowl, complete with geyser jet, would not be out of place on a patio.

A composition for the smallest garden: the tiny fountain from the water lily contrasts with the downward spout from the tortoise.

Fountains *and* Water Spouts

IMAGINATIVE AND UNUSUAL WATER SYSTEMS can easily be introduced into the garden where some focal point is required. In many instances these can be lit for an impressive night time display. For inspiration and ideas, visit a water garden specialist.

Water Pumps

A submersible pump for a fountain or a waterfall is often used for a small pool. It is put on the pool's floor, which must be level, and water is drawn through it to propel the fountain and perhaps supply a waterfall. A waterproof cable then connects it with the electricity supply. A filter in the unit prevents damage caused by debris entering the machine. The flow of water can be adjusted and the form and height of the spray is usually adjustable too.

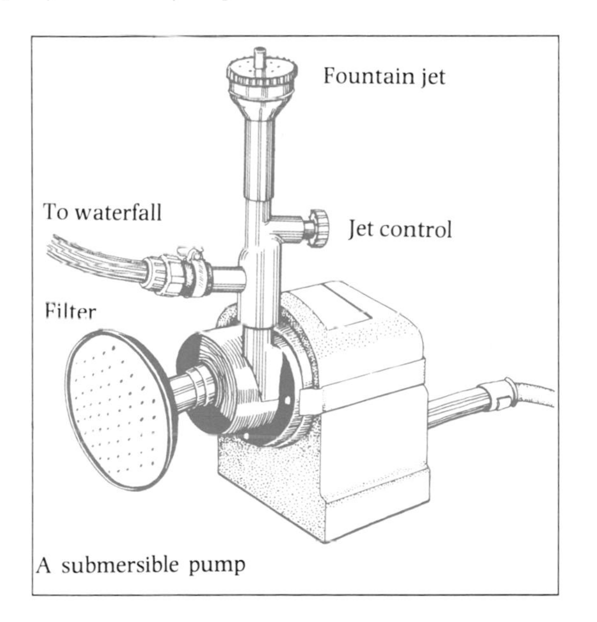

A submersible pump

An elegantly tiered fountain in which the water falls gently over three levels.

◆ *This makes the most of moving vertical lines meeting still horizontals.*

3. Rivers and Streams

Bustling and busy over rocks, smooth and still where the river bed is worn, the little stream journeys onwards through the garden.

BUILDING *a* STREAM

A watercourse can be installed by using a preformed modular unit. Better results are achieved with units that are interlocking rather than assembling different ones which can shift out of place if there is any movement of earth beneath. These two examples show how water pumped to the header pool will cascade down the unit. Plants at the side will quickly blend the units into the landscape.

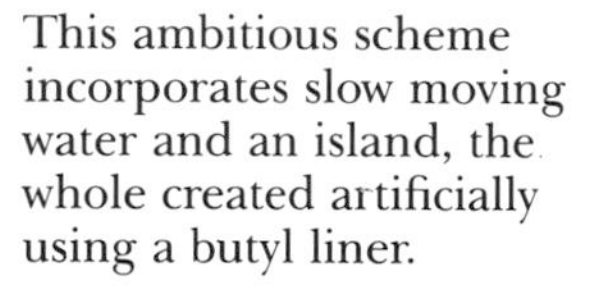

This ambitious scheme incorporates slow moving water and an island, the whole created artificially using a butyl liner.

The head of this small garden stream appears to come from a cleverly constructed rock face.

Building *a* Stream

Modern materials allow for the installation of a stream or water course in most garden situations. Concealing the edges poses the greatest problem. Over-reliance on unmatched rock and stone diminishes the naturalness of the feature and the end result can be disappointing. In nature many streams are found in low-lying wetlands.

The size of your pump is crucial in deciding how long and wide a stream can be when you are building a circulating system.

In this situation an entire water garden has been artfully conceived. Water apparently rises in a small pool built into a little rock garden and then descends along a narrow course to fall finally into an attractively shaped pond. Large boulders have been used to effect and are in sympathy with the flags around the pond. Plantings are appropriate; grass conveys a feeling of space.

BUILDING *a* STREAM

STREAMS, NATURAL OR OTHERWISE, in part concealed, are an inviting feature in the garden when they gently wind an uninterrupted course amongst excesses of plantings, the water in places barely perceptible, just audible.

The sound of this babbling brook would be audible from the painted bridge.

Lysichiton americanus (Skunk cabbage) makes a spring show beside a stream. Large leaves follow the flower spathes.

A newly constructed rivulet made with tiered rock walls on either side. Soil beds between the ranks of stone will allow for planting.

Daffodils naturalize the banks of this wide stretch of water as it travels through the woodland garden.

Springtime, and this water-filled ditch is transformed into a mass of new season's colour.

Water in a grand manner. This beckoning stream passes alongside well furnished banks and among mature trees.

◆ *Although this scale is inappropriate for a small garden a similar atmosphere could be created in a smaller space.*

Despite the small waterfall this rocky water inlet is becoming choked with duckweed, *Lemna minor*.

An imaginatively designed water feature. Here a narrow stream terminates in a refreshing, well moderated fall.

An elegant narrow watercourse widening in parts into little pools, with simple planting.

◆ *A focal point has been provided in the form of an old wooden seat.*

Planting *a* Bankside

Primula denticulata Drumstick primulas give welcome cheer on this bank. (Beyond, *Myrrhis odorata* begins to flower.) 30 × 30cm/1 × 1ft

Polygonatum multiflorum The arching stems of Solomon's seal have colonized this bankside. ●, 60 × 30cm/2 × 1ft

Narcissus cyclamineus has been planted extensively on this woodland bank to give an early show. 15–20cm/6–8in

Mossy saxifrages, primulas, unfolding ferns and Solomon's seal are all at home at this streamside in spring.

Hosta sieboldiana is seldom out of place. Bold leaves make a strong statement. ◐, 75 × 75cm/2½ × 2½ft

***Leucojum aestivum* 'Gravetye Giant'** Clumps of summer snowflake announce the arrival of spring. 45 × 12cm/ 1½ft × 5in

PLANTING *a* BANKSIDE

BANKSIDES ARE MORE OFTEN THAN NOT FREE-DRAINING and not necessarily, as might be expected, water retentive. This point should be borne in mind when carrying out planting schemes. Although the impression to be given is of lush, damp conditions, these may well have to be contrived. Where the water level is subject to seasonal rise and fall, banks may need to be held up with plants forming strong and extensive root systems. These will knit together to prevent serious erosion.

Geranium endressii Seldom without flower, this is a most accommodating plant for any situation. After flowering, cut hard back to ground level. The plant will quickly renew itself. 60 × 60cm/2 × 2ft

◆ *Many of the hardy geraniums are totally unfussy about site and soil conditions. Flowering over a long period, and of spreading habit, they make excellent subjects for both sunny and shady slopes.*

PLANTING *a* BANKSIDE

A VERSATILE PERENNIAL

Alchemilla mollis (Lady's mantle) is a near faultless, hardy perennial plant, growing to 60 × 60cm/ 2 × 2ft. Totally unconcerned about aspect, site or soil conditions, it will produce sprays of lime-green flowers above glaucous leaves over a long period. After rainfall the prettily shaped leaves hold raindrops in a most appealing manner. To prevent overseeding, remove dying flower spikes. At the same time cut back all leaves to ground level. Within a short period the plant will replenish itself with new, fresh foliage.

Asphodeline lutea (Yellow asphodel) Unusual, rather spiky flowers are set above grassy leaves tinged blue-green. 1m × 60cm/3 × 2ft

Digitalis grandiflora A lovely perennial foxglove thriving in both sun and part shade. Evergreen. 75 × 30cm/2½ × 1ft

Tellima grandiflora is an attractive little evergreen which is most suitable for ground cover in a shady area. 30 × 30cm/1 × 1ft

***Lamium maculatum* 'White Nancy'** A slowly spreading dead nettle with mottled foliage and white flowers. ◐, 30 × 60cm/ 1 × 2ft

◆ *There are also several varieties of dead nettles with pink flowers, such as* L. m. roseum *and* L. m. *'Wootton Pink'.*

Planting *a* Bankside

Bergenia Bold, evergreen leaves of bergenias are invaluable for providing form and interest in the garden. 60 × 45cm/2 × 1½ft

Schizostylis coccinea All Kaffir lilies are best in moist conditions. Flowers appear from late summer. 60 × 30cm/2 × 1ft+

***Dicentra* 'Bacchanal'** All the dicentras look well with water. This one has deep wine-red flowers. 45 × 30cm/1½ × 1ft

Smilacina racemosa Creamy plumes of scented flowers are borne on arching stems throughout the spring. ●, 75 × 75cm/2½ × 2½ft

◆ *Smilacina requires light shade and a lime-free soil.*

***Iris* 'Gerald Darby'** An indispensable iris for its ability to thrive in both dry and damp situations. 1m × 45cm/3 × 1½ft

Gentiana asclepiadea The willow gentian produces sprays of deep blue trumpets in late summer/autumn. Needs moisture. ◐, 1m × 60cm/3 × 2ft

PLANTING *a* BANKSIDE

IN THE WILD the course of a stream is often easily spotted by the line of gnarled willows which line its bank at intervals. So in the garden the incorporation of suitable trees and shrubs into the planting of the bankside will add height as well as valuable year-round structure. Many of the quick-growing willows lend themselves to this role.

Salix helvetica This small grey willow acts as a foil to other plantings.
60 × 60cm/2 × 2ft

◆ *Note the way in which leaves tone with surrounding pebbles.*

***Salix matsudana* 'Tortuosa'** is of particular interest in winter when its twisted branches are most noticeable. 9 × 6m/30 × 20ft

***Salix alba vitellina* 'Britzensis'** Prune this willow severely in spring to encourage the orange-red stems. 1.5 × 1.5m/5 × 5ft+

PLANTING *a* BANKSIDE

Alnus cordata (Italian alder) is well suited to damp situations. Glistening leaves and fruiting cones are a feature. 9 × 6m/30 × 20ft

***Cornus alba* 'Elegantissima'** Variegated leaves on red stems. Hard prune to maintain coloured wood. 2 × 1.5m/6 × 5ft

Sorbaria tomentosa var. ***angustifolia*** (syn. ***aitchisonii***) A suckering shrub with ivory flowers. ◌, 3 × 3m/10 × 10ft

This little stream is given additional depth by the shade cast by cut-leaf acers.

◆ *These cut-leaf Japanese maples make excellent shrubs for a water garden, growing to about 1 × 1.5m/3 × 5ft.*

Originally only known from fossils, from which it was named, the first living specimen of ***Metasequoia glyptostroboides*** was discovered as recently as 1941 in China. A conifer, it is deciduous, its leaves fading to pink and gold in the autumn before they are shed. Plant in moist but well drained soil where it will in time achieve a height in excess of 9m/30ft.

CROSSING POINTS

A slatted bridge as this one is not difficult to construct and is totally functional.

This bridge, used to cross a narrow brook, is little more than an extension of the existing flagged path.

Simple and unobtrusive to fit its setting. A nice touch has been to arch this stone bridge.

This substantial, shaped wooden bridge, dramatically painted Oxford blue, is designed to make a statement.

Surrounding plantings have, in the main, been restricted to green so as not to compete with the bridge.

A notional crossing point to add interest to a tiny Japanese water garden. It is formed from split timbers laid over a curving frame.

The design of this untreated, wooden bridge has been kept deliberately plain in keeping with its surroundings.

Crossing Points

As well as the practical aspect of crossing a river or stream, bridges form a pleasing feature in their own right. Strategically placed, they make a compelling observation platform from which to view other parts of the garden. Wood, iron, stone and brick are all suitable materials with which to construct a bridge. The preferred option will take into account intended style and proposed setting. Timber may be left untreated, stained or painted a sympathetic colour.

In a tiny garden this little water feature of fall, pool and miniature bridge works well. The bridge is not simply a crossing point but also directs the visitor around the garden.

◆ *This is an excellent way of integrating a bridge into the garden – by making it a clear continuation of a path.*

4. Bog Gardens

Moisture-retentive soil which is not allowed to dry out is home to a wide range of interesting and unusual plants.

Creating *a* Bog Garden

An area adjacent to the pond where the soil can be kept permanently damp is an ideal spot to choose for a bog garden. Once established it becomes an extension of a theme and even allows for the possibility of a complete water garden. Using a quality butyl liner, creating a bog garden is approached in much the same way as for a pond. In this case the depth need not necessarily exceed 30cm/1ft. Infill should be of a suitable growing medium. A 'leaking' hose will prevent drying out.

A lush display of foliage and glowing flowers in moist shade.

In this situation the bog garden has been attached to a pond. A retaining wall is constructed to hold back the water on one side, the soil on the other.

A butyl liner here is used to contain a water-retentive medium suitable for the moisture-loving plants that typify the bog garden.

This is a very fine example of a bog garden next to a pond. An early summer show of candelabra primulas surrounds irises and the huge leaves of lysichiton with, on the right, the golden sedge, *Carex elata* 'Aurea'.

◆ *Mown grass acts as a calm green foil to this ebullient planting.*

MASSED PLANTING successfully covers up bare soil during the growing season and discourages the formation of weed seedlings. Careful selection of plant material maintains both colour and interest over a long period.

Polygonum (syn. ***Persicaria***) ***affine*** **'Superbum'** Pink-white flowers become crimson. 20 × 30cm/8in × 1ft

Euphorbia griffithii **'Fireglow'** is teamed here with the pink-flowered polygonum (persicaria). ❍, 1m × 75cm/3 × 2½ft

Euphorbias (spurges) dominate this streamside arrangement. The milky substance within their stems can be harmful to the skin.

Aconitum napellus Indigo-blue flowers are a striking feature in the late summer border. 1.2m × 45cm/ 4 × 1½ft

Candelabra primulas jostle with large-leaved hostas, spiky irises and waving grasses in a deliberate contrast of texture and form. Primulas such as these increase their stock annually by self-seeding.

◆ *Hostas are easily propagated by division. This is best done in the spring as they come into leaf.*

CREATING *a* BOG GARDEN

Hosta The full effect of these superb foliage plants is illustrated here where lime-green contrasts with blue-green. 60–90cm/2–3ft

Pink and white-flowered astilbes grow alongside *Hosta sieboldiana* making effective ground cover. 75 × 75cm/2½ × 2½ft

Arum italicum italicum (syn. ***A. i.*** **'Pictum'**) Wonderfully marbled leaves appear in the autumn. 30 × 30cm/1 × 1ft

Geum **'Red Wings'** An easy plant to raise from seed which will grow in any reasonably rich soil and will reward with a fine floral display in summer. ○, 30 × 30cm/1 × 1ft

◆ *The common name for* Geum *is avens.*

Darmera peltata (Umbrella plant) Following early spring flowers (shown below), shaped leaves develop to cover the ground at the streamside. 1m × 60cm/3 × 2ft

MOISTURE LOVING PLANTS

ASSEMBLED TOGETHER the plants most suited to the conditions of the bog garden compile a formidable collection. Beautiful iris, brazen ranunculus, distinctive primulas, retiring cardamines, exciting lobelias, the list is as varied as it is long.

Iris kaempferi (syn. *I. ensata*) (Japanese flag) A very pretty species which is not difficult to grow. 1m × 60cm/3 × 2ft

Iris missouriensis A fine stand of this most rewarding, lavender-flowered iris originating in the Rocky Mountains. 60 × 60cm/2 × 2ft

◆ *Team these iris with yellow primulas for a colourful show.*

***Iris sibirica* 'Soft Blue'** Siberian flags can grow up to 1.2m/4ft and spread over a large area.

***Iris sibirica* 'Snow Bounty'** Wonderfully white flowers whose falls display zones of deep yellow. 1m × 60cm/ 3 × 2ft

Moisture Loving Plants

Iris setosa Attractive, light green leaves form dense thickets above which are fine purple-toned flowers. 60 × 60cm/2 × 2ft

Cardamine pratensis (Lady's smock) An absolutely delightful flower, opening in early spring. 25 × 10cm/10 × 4ft

Preferring moist soil, members of the *Ranunculus* or buttercup family will thrive anywhere. Seen here with forget-me-nots.

***Lobelia* 'Dark Crusader'** is not fully hardy so in cold regions the crowns should be covered for winter protection. 1m × 30cm/ 3 × 1ft

Primula florindae Citrus-yellow bells have the added bonus of carrying a delicious scent. In flower for many weeks. ◐, 75 × 75cm/2½ × 2½ft

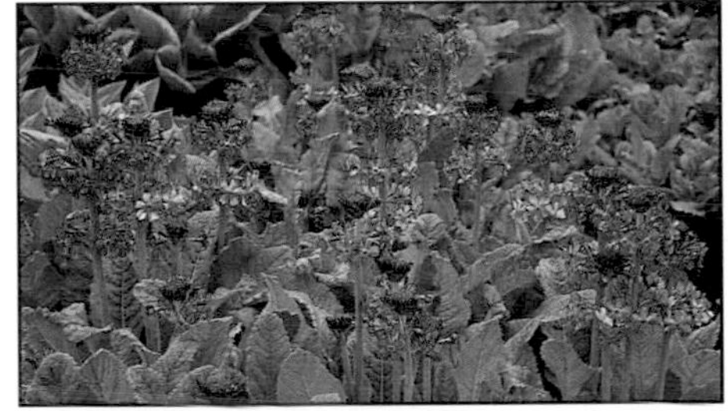

Primula japonica Whorls of pink flowers carried on sturdy stems in early summer. ◐, 45 × 30cm/1½ × 1ft

***Primula* 'Valley Red'** This selected form of candelabra primula is a welcome addition to any garden scene. ◐, 45 × 30cm/1½ × 1ft

Primula vialii Above rosettes of narrow leaves rise cone-shaped lavender flowers, bright scarlet in bud. 30 × 30cm/1 × 1ft

Moisture Loving Plants

The arrangement and positioning of plants in the garden is seldom easy. This is never more so than in the water garden where attention needs to be paid to detail if foliage plants, or those whose flowering period is limited, are to look effective and perform well.

Growing Hostas

Hostas are amongst the most serviceable of foliage plants with their splendid leaves adapting to most planting schemes. Newly emerging shoots in spring can suffer badly from slug damage. To limit this, and avoid an unsightly appearance, top-dress crowns thickly in the early part of the year with a gritty compost mixture. A water-retentive soil and a position out of full sun are essential if hostas are to give of their best. Water during dry periods.

Meconopsis such as these Himalayan blue poppies are not very easy to grow. They require shelter, moist, lime-free soil and a cool aspect. ◐, 1m × 45cm/3 ×1½ft

Trollius europaeus is effective in an unbroken mass. Globe flowers are best divided and transplanted in autumn. 60 × 60cm/2 × 2ft

Senecio tanguticus produces daisy-like yellow flowers in late summer. Fluffy seed heads are an autumn bonus. 1.5m × 60cm/5 × 2ft

Gentiana sino-ornata Bright blue flowers in autumn such as these are hard to resist. For acid soil only. ❍, 15 × 30cm/6in × 1ft

Lysimachia nummularia (Creeping Jenny) spreads to cover a wide area of ground. Sunny blooms are fairly constant. 15cm/6in

In this damp area care has been taken to ensure that leaf shapes contrast with each other.

◆ *The removal of dead flower-heads will keep this composition looking good.*

Moisture Loving Plants

Mimulus The spotted face of this hybrid mimulus is particularly appealing. 30 × 30cm/1 × 1ft

Hot sun has been sufficiently strong to cause the large leaves of *Petasites japonicus* to flop. Plant in shade to avoid this.

Arisaema candidissimum The flower, appearing before the leaves in mid-season, is wonderfully exotic. 30 × 30cm/1 × 1ft

In this garden a sprinkler is set to come on during dry periods. The fine spray is designed not to pan soil but, as far as possible, to imitate natural rainfall. Watering is best carried out early in the morning or in the evening when the loss from evaporation will be much less.

◆ *Avoid surface watering. Water must be enough to penetrate root systems.*

Mixed colours of candelabra primulas can be garish in sun. Here by a shady pool their brilliance is toned down.

◆ *A shaft of sun lights the striped foliage (on the right) of* Iris pseudacorus bastardii.

Moisture Loving Plants

Darmera peltata The umbrella plant is seen in flower here. The leaves have yet to develop. 1m × 60cm/3 × 2ft

Dodecatheon meadia (Shooting star) is a beautiful plant for a damp spot in partial shade. 45 × 30cm/ 1½ × 1ft

Dierama pulcherrimum (Angel's fishing rod) Tall, spraying, evergreen leaves and graceful bell flowers. Up to 1.5 × 1m/5 × 3ft

***Filipendula rubra* 'Venusta'** is a charmingly faded, pink meadowsweet which is spreading, vigorous and easy to grow. 1.5m × 75cm/ 5 × 2½ft

A harmonious and subtle grouping for later summer: astilbes, amongst silver and brown foliage plants.

◆ *The upright plumes of the astilbe and the pendulous brown sedge are an effective contrast.*

GRASSES, SEDGES *and* FERNS

FOR A CONTRAST IN FORM with lower growing plants, the grasses, sedges and taller ferns live up to all expectations. Stirred by the summer breezes they bow their tips together as if sharing some secret. Particularly prized are those with variegation in their slim, dignified leaves.

Osmunda cinnamomea A tall, nicely poised fern refreshingly green in leaf. Unfurling fronds are covered in woolly fluff. 1m × 45cm/3 × 1½ft

Osmunda regalis, the royal fern, will flourish in even quite boggy conditions. Leaves are good for drying. 1.2 × 1.2m/4 × 4ft

Matteuccia struthiopteris The ostrich fern is shown to advantage in generous clumps against a stone path. 1m × 60cm/3 × 2ft

Onoclea sensibilis Although its roots are inclined to run, this fern is suitable for ground cover. 45 × 60cm/ 1½ × 2ft

Adiantum pedatum Exquisite fronds on black wire-like stems. Hardy but enjoys a sheltered spot. 45 × 45cm/1½ × 1½ft

Ferns with very finely cut foliage are to be found in the *Polystichum* group. The fronds of this example are as intricate as lace.

This planting scheme takes advantage of these foliage plants. In the background is ***Miscanthus sinensis* 'Zebrinus'**, a very desirable grass for the way in which the leaves are markedly variegated. In the course of a year this will reach a height of 1.8m/6ft. Centre stage is taken up with ***Matteuccia struthiopteris***, the ostrich fern, whilst at a lower level ***Carex elata*** 'Aurea' (Bowles' golden grass) enjoys the damp conditions. All of these plants should be cut to the ground at the season's end.

Cool, elegant and diverse, the ferns deserve to be brought back from the obscurity into which they have passed in recent times. A lightly shaded, moist site is where they are happiest. In spring their unfolding fronds are an absolute delight.

GRASSES, SEDGES *and* FERNS

SOME SEDGES AND GRASSES will, if given free reign, become somewhat invasive, romping beyond the boundaries set for them. These are best avoided in the smaller garden, although routine maintenance should check their enthusiasm. Others are most garden-worthy and merit seeking out.

Typha angustifolia (Bulrush) should be included wherever space permits. Handsome poker seed heads are most striking. 1.8m/6ft

Stipa tenuifolia Wispy seedheads and graceful form recommend this grass for cultivation. ❍, 60 × 45cm/2 × 1½ft

◆ *Architectural grasses like this can play an important part in most garden borders.*

***Carex elata* 'Aurea'** This sedge is at its best in midsummer when its arching stems are golden. 60 × 60cm/2 × 2ft

Carex pendula (Pendulous sedge) contrasts well with other foliage plants. Shade tolerant and self-seeding. 1.2 × 1m/4 × 3ft

GRASSES, SEDGES *and* FERNS

The colour of this sedge is most intense in winter. Frosted, it looks terrific.

***Carex comans* (bronze form)** is used here to soften the edges of a gravel path. 60 × 60cm/2 × 2ft

***Phalaris arundinacea* 'Picta'** Gardeners' garters is undoubtedly attractive for its conspicuous variegation. It is, however, invasive. 1.2m/4ft

***Spartina pectinata* 'Aureomarginata'** is an elegant grass for moist soil in a situation where it has room to spread. 1.8m/6ft

◆ *Green flower spikes are hung with massed stamens of purple.*